GOD'S SOVEREIGNTY AND FREE MORAL AGENCY

GOD'S SOVEREIGNTY AND FREE MORAL AGENCY

how both truths are biblically consistent

J. R. GRAVES

Peter Lumpkins

Free Church Press Voices of the Free Church

Copyright © 2020 by *Free Church Press*

All rights reserved. No part of this book may be reproduced in any manner whatsoever without written permission except in the case of brief quotations embodied in critical articles and reviews.

First Printing, 2020

To Emir Caner and Ergun Caner,
faithful brothers in Christ
and
unkillable voices
of the
Free Church tradition

Contents

Dedication — v

Preface — 1

1. About J. R. Graves — 4
2. Introduction — 10
3. PROPOSITION I — 14
4. PROPOSITION II — 26
5. PROPOSITION III — 34

Preface

Free Church Press is honored to offer this short compilation by James Robinson "J.R." Graves (1820-1893). Graves served as editor of *The Tennessee Baptist* beginning in 1848 and served several decades until his death in 1893 (see About J.R. Graves).

The selections deal with Graves' understanding of the relationship of God's sovereignty and human free will and are taken *as published* in three consecutive editions in 1848—January 27, February 3, and February 17, respectively. No overt attempt has been made to correct grammatical errors unless clarity was at stake. Nor was there need to insert either commentary or footnotes. One of Graves' most evident gifts was his ability to persuade the masses as his paper's wide circulation so amply attests.

Each article was originally published as three propositions. Though the Introduction was originally published at the beginning of Proposition I, by editorial decision, it is printed separate from Proposition I in this volume. We trust no breach in the context occurred while clarity prevailed.

A note should be included to expand briefly on what was suggested above--an absence of critical commentary on these short articles especially in light of the contentious nature of the subject. As stated elsewhere, the intellectual wrestling over God's sovereignty and human free will has gained the attention of both theologian and philosophers for centuries, millenniums even. And given there appears as much argument over the compatibility or incompatibility between the two propositions as yesteryear, it seems to follow that no one has yet proposed an argument so compelling on either side as to lay the issue to rest.

Consequently, it should not be assumed that a mere three articles in a denominational newspaper written for mass consumption was, or is now, presented as the last word, so to speak, on the subject. Free Church Press does not think so. Indeed it remains most probable that not even J.R. Graves, were he alive today, would so boldly claim!

So while Graves reasons soundly and interprets properly many passages of Scripture in these short articles, some readers undoubtedly will discover places where he falls short in his presentation. We expect thinking Christians to critically engage Graves' works like any other works, especially judging his conclusions in light of biblical revelation--our final, sufficient, and unerring standard in determining truth.

Like all men, J.R. Graves was a man with feet of clay. He did not get all his theology right (nor do we). Nonetheless, Graves was a giant in evangelical circles for half a century. He influenced tens of thousands of believers in their walk with Christ. And most significantly, Graves preached the gospel all over the United States leading untold numbers to faith in Christ to save them from sin.

Thus, it remains an honor to reproduce a brief but helpful compilation of writings from the pen of J.R. Graves.

I

About J. R. Graves

James Robinson Graves was born in Chester, Vermont on April 10, 1820. His father died a mere two weeks after J.R. was born. Though Mrs. Graves was heir to her husband's prosperous business, her late husband's partner was unscrupulous and shrewd enough to cheat her out of her husband's estate. Consequently, J.R. grew up with means enough to garner not even a basic education.

Not content J.R. began a rigorous process of self-education which included learning a different foreign language each year for four consecutive years. Though Graves was reared in the Congregational church tradition, he soon joined a Baptist church in Ohio where his family moved when he was 19. After moving to Kentucky a few years later, the Mount Freedom Baptist Church in Nicholasville ordained J.R. to the gospel ministry.

The young Graves moved to Nashville, Tennessee in 1845 to take a teaching position and subsequently joined the First Baptist Church. Graves then served as pastor for a short time before becoming a junior editor for *The Baptist* (at other times, *The Tennessee Baptist*) which was the denominational newspaper for several southern states and whose Chief Editor was Graves' former pastor at Nashville's First Baptist Church, R.B.C. Howell. Howell resigned as Chief Editor three years later, and J.R. was made Chief Editor in Howell's place, an appointment that would eventually catapult J.R. Graves to become one who, in the words of one historian, "influenced Southern Baptist life of the 19th century in more ways, and probably in a greater degree, than any other person." (Note: Graves would later experience a tragic estrangement from Howell, an estrangement that would lead to Graves being excommunicated from First Baptist Church.)

With a readership exceeding 12,000, Graves influenced the opinions of Baptists in the south on a wide range of issues in culture, theology, local church, and denominational life for several decades as editor. During these years, Graves preached all over the United States. Reportedly, he possessed a magnetic persona in the pulpit and was incredibly persuasive in speech. As a debater, he practiced a scorched-earth approach toward his opponents and became a Baptist favorite to go after Methodist and Church of Christ advocates. Graves' reputation earned from the "father" of the Restoration Movement (Church of Christ), Alexander Campbell, this scathing description:

> *This gentleman, if I may so abuse the word, is one of the best definitions of total depravity, in a living and formal development of the term, that, under the Christian profession, in an experience of 40 years, I have been made acquainted with.*

GOD'S SOVEREIGNTY AND FREE MORAL AGENCY - 7

Moreover, Graves served not only as editor of the Tennessee paper, but he also established Nashville's Southwestern Publishing House and pursued production of books decidedly favorable to Baptist history and heritage.

Even so, perhaps J.R. Graves' most memorable influence is his association with the Landmark Movement among Baptists. Historians suggest that the Landmark Movement officially began at Cotton Grove Baptist Church outside of Jackson, Tennessee on June 24, 1851 inspired by an address Graves spoke to a packed house. In short, the Landmark Movement insisted the Baptist Church is not *closest* to the church one finds in the New Testament. Rather the Baptist church *is* the church found in the New Testament, the *only* church the Apostles established. While there are other nuances of Landmarkism, this particular claim strikes at the heart of Landmark ecclesiology. Some critics suggested (perhaps unfairly) Landmarkism reduced Baptists to a Protestant version of the Catholic Church.

Consequently, J.R. Graves might well be considered the "father" of Landmarkism. Yet Graves was not the only one who possessed a powerful influence over Baptists in the south and southwest concerning Landmarkism.

Kentucky pastor and Union University professor, James Madison Pendleton (1811-1891), penned one of the most influential tracts on Landmarkism—*An Old Landmark Reset*—that answered the question in the negative, "Ought Baptists to recognize Pedobaptist preachers as ministers of the Gospel?" Pendleton was invited by Graves to answer the question in a series of articles in the *Tennessee Baptist* in 1854. The articles were subsequently published as the tract. Graves and Pendleton, along with another influential Baptist layman, A. C. Dayton (1813-1865), a dentist and member of Nashville's First Baptist Church, became known as the "Great Triumvirate" (Dayton was subsequently excommunicated along with Graves over Graves' controversy with the church's pastor, R.B.C. Howell).

Through the influence of these three men, particularly J.R. Graves, Landmarkism swallowed a large swath of Baptist churches across the south lasting well into the 20th century. Landmark advocates formed national networks including the Missionary Baptist General Association (later the

American Baptist Association), Kentucky-Tennessee General Association of Gospel Mission Churches, and the Baptist Missionary Association of America.

While Landmarkism is not as prominent as it was at the end of the 19th century when J.R. Graves passed on to his eternal reward (1893), his signature influence still lives on in conservative Baptist circles over a century later.

Peter Lumpkins, Editor
Cleveland, Georgia
Fall 2020

2

Introduction

Discourse delivered at Courtland, Alabama, Introductory to the Union Meeting July 2d, and subsequently preached at the Duck River Association, 1841, by J.R. Graves, Pastor of the 2nd Baptist Church, Nashville, Tenn.

THY WILL BE DONE—*Lord's Prayer*

We are convinced of no one thing, better than, that disappointments and affliction are our lot as mortals. We [inherit] them with our earthly being. Many of our disappointments and much of our unhappiness are the result of our own improvidence, and recklessness—while other afflictions are dispensed by the hand of God. The former should teach us wisdom, the latter submission. We should always discriminate between the providences sent by God, and the results of our own rash actions. The former we should bear with great meekness, and resignation, knowing that it is our Father in Heaven, who doeth all things well. The prayer of the afflicted child of God will ever be, "Thy will be done."

We might devote, and profitably too, the present hour, in considering these dispensations, and our duty under them—but the occasion, and this large assembly, will warrant a more extended discourse.

Before entering upon the discussion of our text, a question naturally arises, why should we pray that God's will may be done, when we read in Dan. iv: 35, that "he doeth according to his will in the armies of heaven, and among the inhabitants of earth, and none can stay his hand, or say unto him, what doest thou?"

If this means that his will, taken in any, or

every sense, will be done by him, irrespective of any thing that man can do, why should we pray for its accomplishment? But we find that his will, taken in some sense, is not done, unless all men are finally saved, for Paul speaking of God says, 1 Tim. ii: 4. "Who will have all men to be saved and come to the knowledge of the truth." Now if all men are saved, it must be irrespective of their moral character, which would involve a gross absurdity, and oppose the whole tenor of the New Testament. There evidently is a distinction between the term *will*, in these two passages. The will of God is taken in scripture,

1. For his absolute purpose—his *irresistible operations.*
2. His precepts, and commands. God's *purposing will* is the rule of *his* conduct. His *commanding* will, the rule of *ours.*

God's purposing will, is exercised and accomplished, in all things pertaining to his universal government, both, as relates to the army of heaven and among the inhabitants of the earth, in carrying out his designs. For the accomplishment of this will he commands us not to pray.

His commanding will—his pleasure, has reference to man's allegiance to his: government, and filial obedience, love and duty to him as a sovereign. This he commands, but leaves it optional with man to obey, or disobey, to choose, or refuse, placing the reward and penalty before him, to influence him in the decision.

Having defined our terms, we will now proceed "to the height of this great argument...[to] assert eternal providence. And to justify the ways of God to man."

3

PROPOSITION I

God's absolute will or purposes has reference to his own sovereign acts, in the creation and government of his universe, the rise and fall of kingdoms and empires, etc., and the execution of his purposes in the earth, irrespective of what man can do, but in such a manner as not to infringe upon man's *moral agency*, i.e. as respects his love to him, or his acceptance or rejection of the benefits of the *atonement*.

God by his own sovereignty, created all the worlds of his boundless dominion—gave laws to planets and sun, and after the counsel of his own will established governments for their intelligences. No reader of revelation will deny this, and it involves eternal purpose. Foreknowledge, predestination and election. May it not be the misunderstanding, and misapplication of these terms, that produced such contrariety of doctrinal views? It seems that if the proper order of these terms was preserved, and their relative bearing borne in mind, that mountains of difficulties would immediately disappear.

The terms that perplex this subject, are Ordination, Decrees, Immutable Will, Foreknowledge, Election, Predestination, &c. The order in which we would arrange them is,

1. Foreknowledge.
2. Predestination, predetermination or purpose.
3. Decrees.
4. Election or Choice.
5. Ordination or pleasure, will—desire.

Let us illustrate. So far as man *foresees*, he purposes or predetermines, or predestines his own acts, and the acts of those under his commands. These determinations expressed, (as do Kings) become his *"decrees,"* or commands. He chooses or elects the *means and time* of their accomplishment; i.e. how, by whom, under what circumstances, and when they shall be brought about, —all this concerns the transaction of his own plans and business.

2. He fixes or ordains rules for his servants and children to observe, both towards him and among themselves. 1. That they should not only obey, but revere, respect and love him, and 2. That they should pay due regard to the rights and feelings, and love one another. The first, that which has strict reference to his own acts he can perform, but the 2nd, which has reference to the acts of others, acts which he cannot compel, he cannot in all instances cause to be done. This is all simple and easy of comprehension. Let us apply this illustration to [illuminate] our subject.

1. God sees from Alpha to Omega, the end as well as the beginning—he can learn nothing—all time to him, is one present now. Suppose God to act in this respect, as we do, i.e. to determine our actions so far as we foresee, he must have pre-

determined or purposed all his own acts, *from all eternity*, because *foreseeing, or foreknowing all things from all eternity*. When he declares his predeterminations, or purposes—they become, his immutable decrees. The choosing or electing of the means for the accomplishment of his decrees, is his election or choice. All this has reference to his own acts in the administration of his government—the affairs of the world—in its phases, physical, political and spiritual—the rise and fall of empires and kingdoms, potentates or rulers—all this he does after the counsel of his own will, and "none can stay his hand, or say, what doest thou."

2. But God ordains-desires-wishes-wills-that all his children should revere, obey, and love him supremely, and each love his fellow as himself. This he cannot always, can but seldom do, for he cannot *force a man to love* nor compel a *moral* being to *obey*. This will, or desire of God we should labor and pray might "be done on earth as in heaven,"—that it might as God desires become the rule of our conduct.

Let us briefly notice some of the acts of sovereignty.

1. He, according to his own purpose, because

he foresaw from the beginning it was best, created this earth for the abode of rational, moral beings—*free moral agents*, capable of discriminating, and with the power of choosing between good and evil. He foresaw their fall and its consequences, from creating them thus; but we are at a loss to see how he could create rational beings, without making them at the same time accountable, and if accountable, they must be *free moral* agents. All the intelligences of his universe—in earth or heaven, are subjects of *law*. Law implies rationality—rewards and penalty imply freedom of choice—unforced obedience, or disobedience.

If God compelled, by irresistible motives, the obedience of men or angels, he could not reward such service—if he forced disobedience by irresistible motives he could not punish—but he either rewards [or] punishes all his created intelligences; therefore it follows—

1. They are accountable.
2. They are free moral agents.
3. The obedience of no one is forced.
4. The disobedience of no one is forced.

GOD'S SOVEREIGNTY AND FREE MORAL AGENCY

Consequently, man loves or hates God because he chooses to do so. The Armenian meets here with this argument. "If God *foresees* a transaction, will it not as necessarily take place as though he had decreed it?" Well, we all know that to be omniscient, (which attribute he must possess to be God) he must have foreknown or foreseen all things.

> *as God of all*
> *A hero perish or a sparrow fall,*
> *Atoms as kingdoms into ruin hurled,*
> *And now a bubble burst, and now a world*

It becomes us both to seek an answer to stop the mouth of the fatalist, rather than quarrel about the matter of a *fixed and revealed fact*. Milton has expressed himself better than we can hope to do. He represents God as saying of Adam after the fall.

Ingrate! He had of me
All he could have: I made him just and right.
Sufficient to have stood, though free to fall,
Such I created all the ethereal powers
And spirits both them who stood, and them who fell,
Freely they stood who stood, and fell who fell.
Not free, what proof could they have given sincere.
Of true allegiance, constant faith and love.
When only what they needs must do appeared
Not what they would? What praise could they receive?
What pleasure I from such allegiance paid?
When will and reason (reason also is choice,)
Useless and vain, of freedom both despoiled
Made passive both; had served necessity
Not me. They therefore as to right belonged,
So were created, nor can justly accuse
Their Maker, or their making or their fate.
As if predestination overruled.
Their will, disposed by absolute decree

GOD'S SOVEREIGNTY AND FREE MORAL AGENCY

Or high foreknowledge; They themselves decreed
Their own revolt, not I. If I foreknew
Foreknowledge had no influence on their fault.
Which had no less proved certain unknown
So without least impulse or shadow of fate
They trespassed—authors to themselves in all
Both what they judge and what they choose."

Did you commit a sin last week, or last year? and did not God foresee years ago, that you would? Whom do you blame, yourself or God? Would you not have done the same act, had God not foreseen? Again, did not God foresee years ago, how many bales of cotton or barrels of corn you would raise this year? Would you have raised less, or more if he had not foreknown? Was it not, after all, dependent upon your own exertions? Would you have reaped if you had not sown?

We infer, 1. That God does foreknow or foresee, and 2. That this foreseeing does not *force* our will to choose or refuse salvation. To return, 1. God foresaw the ruin entailed by the fall, he foresaw the means by which man could be redeemed from its curse. Here is God's *foreknowledge*. 2. He determines or purposes to adopt it, —here is his eternal and immutable purpose, *predestination*. 3. He declares this purpose, —here is his eternal *decree*. 4. He makes choice of the means, "the seed of the woman shall bruise the serpent's head;" the person—his own son, the time and circumstances—who shall announce his coming, and who shall be his Apostles,—here we see God's sovereign, unconditional, personal and particular election. To be more particular.

Christ is to be made of a woman—made under the *law*. Now some particular nation must be chosen, from which he is to spring, and through which the knowledge and the blessings of this sacrifice can be brought nigh and enjoyed. Of all the patriarchs of the east, Abram is chosen. Why he was elected in preference to Melchesedek, none can tell. Abram has two sons, Isaac and Ishmael, Isaac is chosen. Isaac has two sons, Esau and Jacob, Jacob is chosen in preference to Esau, which is the meaning of that scripture, "Jacob have I loved and Esau have I hated," though Esau seems to be the better character of the two. Here is particular, personal election. Jacob has twelve sons, these are chosen to be the progenitors of a large and peculiar nation. Twelve, and not thirteen was God's favorite number.

Let us notice another eternal purpose of God. He foresaw that it was necessary or fit that this chosen people should suffer a cruel bondage, and then to be brought out of it with an outstretched hand, in order to impress most forcibly his glorious attributes upon their minds and memories to the latest generations. *Foreseeing* this, he determines or purposes it.

3. He declares this purpose, —this is his decree. We read it in Gen. xv: 13. "Know of a surety that thy seed shall be a stranger in a strange land, and shall serve them, and they shall afflict them 400 years, and also that nation whom they serve will I judge, and afterwards they shall come out with great substance." Now this was God's decree, made known hundreds of years before its accomplishment, and it must needs come to pass just as he determined it. He accordingly elects or chooses

the means, i.e. time, persons, nation, and circumstances.

In due time, Joseph is sold into Egypt—God preserves and raises him to a second place in the kingdom. Famine is brought upon the land.

This brings, ultimately, Jacob and his family into Egypt, when he is finally enslaved. At the expiration of the 400 years Moses is born, preserved, raised and educated a prince. God reveals his purpose to him—and finally redeems Israel, overthrowing Pharaoh in the sea. The descendants of the twelve sons become a great nation divided into twelve tribes, —from one of these tribes is the Messiah to be born. Judah is chosen. From all the families of Judah, Jesse's family is selected, of all his sons David, of all David's sons Solomon, —and when the time had fully come, when Christ should appear, of all the villages of Judea, Bethlehem is chosen, and of all the virgins of the line of Jesse, Mary alone "found grace in the sight of the Lord" to be the mother of Emanuel.

Thus, have we seen, by simply tracing along one event, eternal, absolute, particular, unconditional, personal election, which no one can deny. God determining to bring it about, none could

GOD'S SOVEREIGNTY AND FREE MORAL AGENCY

"stay his hand"—he governed and controlled the circumstances which brought it all forward, just as he willed it. It all pertained to his *sovereignty*, and he accomplished it. Christ died by the determinate will and purpose of God—to bring in a new and better covenant which God decreed from the beginning, and is it not rational to suppose that he, from the beginning, also fixed, determined or decreed the conditions of that covenant in and through which lost man might be saved? We have thus far seen that God can act the part of a sovereign, rule and direct his own affairs, without infringing upon the *moral* will of the creature, i.e. compel the creature to love, or hate him.

To be continued.

4

PROPOSITION II

God predestinates, raises up and elects certain persons, to perform certain parts in the drama of nations, and he irresistibly inclines their wills or hearts to do his pleasure, in these respects, but in no wise compelling any to love or hate him, so as to be saved or lost.

First, God raised up Moses to receive his law and to lead the Children of promise out of the land of bondage, and appointed Aaron to be a mouth unto him, and all their acts (save their moral acts) were by the purpose and determinate

GOD'S SOVEREIGNTY AND FREE MORAL AGENCY - 27

will of God, he influencing their wills to do them. Yet did this necessarily compel them to be saved or lost—did it deter them from sin? By no means, for we behold the meek Moses angry before the Rock, and devout Aaron making a golden calf for the idolatry of Israel, and neither entered the Promised land. If God had compelled their moral acts, irresistibly forced or inclined their hearts to love, or hate him, no blame or sin could have rested upon them, and they could not have been justly forbidden to enter Canaan.

2. Pharaoh is another proof of this fact. "For this same purpose have I raised thee up," for what? to hate him? No, but "that I might show my power in thee, and that my name might be declared throughout all the earth." The term, "raised up"—*exegeira* [sic]— means also to preserve. How many times Pharaoh, like other wicked kings, had deserved the severest judgments of God and to be cut off from the land of the living, but God *"preserved him* to punish him in a more public and striking manner," he even *"raised him* up to the throne of Egypt," and made him king in place of his brother. His design in this was to strike fear and awe into all the nations and kings of the whole

earth. Any punishment brought upon him as a private individual would not do this, therefore God preserved him, and finally raised him to the throne, and when the time that he had fixed had fully come, *God* hardened his heart, and caused him to follow, at the head of his forces, the Israelites into the Sea, and there he overthrew him miraculously, and filled the nations with awe and reverence, for the Jehovah of Israel. I do not see any injustice in God's hardening the heart of Pharaoh, in order to bring him to a certain end. His sins were the *cause* of his death—God had a right to select the *manner* of it. He did so, and magnified his own name by the destruction of this monster of iniquity, and thus, as it were, repaid himself for his long forbearance. Many an Israelite passed that Sea, who deserved to share the fate of Pharaoh, but God had compassion and preserved them, and when his goodness only hardened them in wickedness and crime, he overthrew them in the desert. We find here a comment upon that passage. "Therefore he will have mercy on whom he will have mercy, and whom he will, he hardeneth."

3. Cyrus is another instance we could adduce in the support of our proposition, that God pre-

destinates the acts that shall be accomplished, and elects certain men and irresistibly influences their wills to perform them. Certain kingdoms and nations of the east are to be overthrown, and the pride of Babylon to be subdued, and her wickedness punished. This is God's *purpose;* he declares it by the mouth of his prophet—it then becomes his *decree.* He elects the means, i.e. the *person, time* and *circumstances.* God elects Cyrus, and for this purpose, calls him by name, marks out his course, and declares his acts, 200 years before he was born.

1. To Overthrow Babylon

"Thus saith the Lord to his anointed, to Cyrus whose right hand I have holden to subdue nations before him; and I will loose the loins of kings, to open before him the two-leaved gates, and the gates shall not be shut. I will go before thee, and make the crooked straight; I will break in pieces the gates of brass, and cut asunder the bars of iron &c.—Vide Isa. 45: 1-7.

2. To Build Jerusalem.

"Of Cyrus, he is my shepherd, and shall perform all my pleasure, even saying to Jerusalem, Thou shalt be built, and to the temple thy foundation shall be laid."—Isa. 44: 28

"I have raised him up in righteousness, and *I will direct all his ways*, he shall build my city, and he shall let go my captives not for price or reward, saith the Lord of Hosts."

Read the history of Cyrus as recorded by historians, and we shall find, that Cyrus performed all these acts as God predicted, but did all this, though God influenced and enabled him to do it, compel him to love God and secure his salvation? or to reject him and effect his condemnation? Not in the least. See how clearly the history of Alexander is written by the pen of Prophecy, in Dan. 8:1-8. "The Macedonian kingdom is represented under the figure of a He Goat, and the King as a notable horn—between the eyes. And he came to the ram that had two horns, [i.e. the empire of the Medes and Persians] and broke them, and when he was strong [i.e. the Macedonian power after the conquest of the east,] the great horn [Alexander] was broken and for it came up four notable ones, towards the four winds of heaven."—Alexander's kingdom was divided between his four generals.

The prophecy in regard to Cesar, and Bonaparte, might be adduced for proof, but it is not

GOD'S SOVEREIGNTY AND FREE MORAL AGENCY - 31

necessary. We *know* these characters were designed for the accomplishment of certain purposes, because God revealed the fact by the mouth of his Prophets. But did he not determine the course, and acts of any other individual save those of whom prophecy speaks? The inference is clear that he does mark out the acts and sphere of every other man—still *leaving his moral acts unforced.* Who can doubt but that Columbus, was impressed and guided from above to find in another hemisphere a hiding place for the persecuted church of God, or that our own Washington was raised up by God to lead our armies forth to battle for Liberty, and that he was guided and shielded by the same Almighty hand from the snares of his enemies, and from every weapon formed against him. But this did not compel Washington to become a Christian or an infidel. It might be asked. "How far can God influence my actions, and not destroy my accountability?" Just so far as a master can influence or command the action or services of a servant, and not interfere with his accountability to God, and even more, for the master has no power over his life, and [sic] God has over ours. He fixes the day of our birth and appoints the number of our days, which we cannot pass.

"Seeing his days are *determined*, and the *number* of his months are with thee, thou hast appointed his bounds that he *cannot pass*." Then all my actions God may control save my moral actions, and my accountability be not in the least impaired.

He determined the day of my birth —my parentage, whether obscure or highly honorable—the amount of natural powers with which I am endowed, advantages of development. He determined my nation—whether civilized or barbarous, religious or pagan—and my sphere of action. All men are called or elected, to fill some definite sphere—one to the study of medicine, one to the practice of law, another to the arts and others to preach the gospel, and why men do not succeed better in their several pursuits and are not happier, is because they do not the will of God in this respect—do not obey their calling. No doubt many a physician should preach—and many who are trying to preach should make shoes or till the earth.

Thus, we see that the Almighty presides in general over all events which happen in the world;

GOD'S SOVEREIGNTY AND FREE MORAL AGENCY

and rules with absolute sway, the fate of all men in particular, of all cities, and of all empires; but he conceals the operations of his wisdom, and the wonders of his providence beneath the veil of natural causes and ordinary events. God seems to have no concern in these things and we should be tempted to believe that he abandons men entirely to their views, their talents and their passions, did he not, to prevent a belief so repugnant to religion and even to reason itself, occasionally break the silence, disperse the clouds, and discover to us the secret springs of his providence, by causing his prophets to foretell, long before the event, 'the fate he has prepared for the different nations of the earth. Yet all in strict accordance with equity and justice.

To It continued

5

PROPOSITION III

So far as relates to the eternal salvation of the human family in general, God has eternally determined and decreed that it shall be through the unforced belief of the truth, and obedience to God.

God has proved by the gift of his Son and his long-suffering towards sinners, that he is unwilling that *any* should perish, but that *all* should come to repentance. Far from influencing any to choose destruction and death,—all his acts, and every motive drawn from the realities of three

GOD'S SOVEREIGNTY AND FREE MORAL AGENCY - 35

worlds—every means he can consistently use, he does put forth for man's salvation—every act of his goodness leading to repentance—all the gentle wooings of the spirit drawing to Christ—surely if men were moved by the strongest motives they would all accept of the inestimable benefits of atonement through Christ.

The doctrine of eternal and unconditional election, and reprobation as taught by Calvin and assented to by many professed Christians, we utterly repudiate—it finds no place in our faith or affections. It is as contrary to our reason as to our understanding of the Word of God. If God did eternally predestinate, elect and decree the final salvation of a definite number of persons, A, B, and C, irrespective of their future *moral* character or acts, and did also decree the final damnation of D, E, and F, or "all the rest not elected to life," irrespective of their future moral character or acts, then it follows that

Either he will save some, who *disbelieve* the truth, and damn some who love our Lord Jesus Christ.

Or he must *invincibly* force some to love him and some to hate him, so that he might damn them. Both of which suppositions are contrary to the plain construction and spirit of the Bible, and effectually destroys all human accountability and *moral* agency. For nothing is plainer to human reason than that *forced* obedience could not be rewarded—or forced disobedience be punished. It would be the same should God govern our actions by the stronger motives. It is granted that God *could* throw before creatures *invincible* motives, so as to govern and control all our now moral acts, but they would lose their *moral* character, as palpably as though he had made use of *physical* instead of *motive force*. It would in either case be *force* which is incompatible with a moral government.

Now so far as we are informed, God's election is always according to *foreknowledge*. "Elect according to the foreknowledge of God." 1 Peter 1: 2. If God is omniscient all his acts must be according to foreknowledge. If God elected all who are finally saved according to his foreknowledge, it must be that he elected to be saved, such as he foreknew would believe the truth, or such as he foresaw would reject it, either of which would be an election of *character* not *persons*, which fact we are compelled to believe. But can it be that he elected to eternal life

GOD'S SOVEREIGNTY AND FREE MORAL AGENCY

those whom he foresaw or foreknew would finally *reject* the truth and *hate* Christ? Or did he dispossess himself for the time of his omniscience, close his eyes, and decree a certain *quantity*, instead of a certain character for salvation? Impossible for *eternal wisdom* thus to act. What would you think of that man, before whom was set a large measure full of gold coins and pieces of tin of the same size, and being freely all he chose, should instead carefully selecting the gold, should shut his eyes and be satisfied with clutching a handful of whatever kind it might be! Would an infinitely wise God thus discern between the righteous and the wicked?

We believe that 1st, God foresaw the fall—not that he decreed the fall, for he has not chosen to decree *moral actions*, only the *consequences* of moral acts.

2nd He determined and purposed to bring in a remedy.

3rd He declared this purpose, and it became his decree.

4th He elected the means. "The seed of the woman shall bruise the serpent's head," person, his own Son— time and circumstances.

This was done from before the foundation of

the world. He at the same time determined terms or conditions of man's acceptance and justification. These predetermined terms have been published to the world, by the mouths of his prophets, and lastly by his Son, and thus have passed into a decree. And what is God's eternal decree and predestination upon this subject? I answer, "He that believeth and is baptized shall be saved, and he that believeth not shall be damned." God has chosen to know, in his purposes of grace only a *character*—not a person, or a certain *quantity*, and that character is the BELIEVER. If God has only decreed the final salvation of believers, he has only *elected* believers to salvation, for he elects or chooses *according* to his decrees, not *contrary* to them. We therefore conclude that all those who believe on Christ are eternally, in the mind and purpose of God elected unto life, and all those who reject the counsels and grace of God against themselves, are eternally decreed to everlasting condemnation. God in no way, invincibly forcing any to choose or reject his mercy.

One may ask, "Was I not elected from all eternity a child of God? As a character you were. As one whom God foresaw, would accept the truth, you were in his mind elected or chosen to salvation, he determining at the same time, that you should become conformed to the image of his Son—by that conformation to be justified—sanctified—glorified. Every one that ever was saved, or ever will be saved, is thus foreknown, predestinated, elected, called or justified, sanctified, and glorified, in the eternal mind of the Deity, from all eternity. It becomes personal and known to us when we accept provisions of the atonement. We do not *merit* any thing by accepting the terms of mercy, no more than the beggar by accepting the alms we give to save him from starvation. We do not purchase salvation by the performance of the conditions. "By grace are ye saved, through faith, and that not of yourselves, it is the gift of God, not of works lest any man should boast."

The Calvinist here offers his objections.

"You must grant that all will be saved for whom Christ died, else the designs of his death will be frustrated. Now he either died for a definite—elect, number or for the whole world in general. If it was for the whole family of man, then all will be saved, which must be false, therefore he must have died for a definite number only, which is the elect."

Now we grant no such thing, there is sophistry in this reasoning. It mistakes the true nature of the atonement, and reasons from two absurdities, i.e. from a limited and unlimited view of the atonement.

Christians are divided upon the atonement. Calvinists or limited atonement men, and Arminian, or unlimited atonement. We regard these as two extremes. We profess to be neither a Calvinist nor an Arminian, but look for truth between the two. Those who support a limited atonement quote such passages as these: "I lay down my life for the sheep"; "the church of God which he hath purchased with his own blood," &c.; while those who oppose it with an universal atonement, quote such passages as these: "a ransom for all,"; "the Saviour of all men," "he died for all,"; "he tasted death for every man." Now both doctrines cannot be supported in the light these sects view it, or the Bible contradicts itself. There must be a *sense* in which all these expressions, and many others can be reconciled.

We understand the scriptures to teach that the

death or sacrifice of Christ has reference to two things. 1. In reference to God. 2. For believers.

What it accomplished in reference to God, was to enable him "to be just and yet the justifier of him that believeth in Jesus," i.e. that God might consistently with his law and holy character, become propitious to sinners. In this sense Christ died for all, and the atonement unlimited—made for all, and all men are invited by the spirit and the Bride to come and partake of its benefits.

2. What it designed to accomplish for believers, is "the power to become the sons of God," i.e. that every sheep that trusts itself to the keeping of this shepherd of their souls, shall be everlastingly saved from every foe—be one ultimately with him, and behold his glory. In this sense it is limited, for none but believers will be benefited by it.

We might be asked again, "Did Christ offer himself without any fixed purpose? Did he die and leave it all to chance whether his death should prove in vain or not?" We answer, He did not. The Everlasting Father gave him assurance that his death should be efficacious and by the sacrifice of himself many would be justified. "By his knowledge shall my righteous servant justify many, for he shall bear their iniquities." "When thou shalt make his soul an offering for sin, he shall see his seed, he shall prolong his days, and the pleasure of the Lord shall prosper in his hand." "He shall see of the travail of his soul and shall be satisfied." The certainty of the salvation of one soul, would have caused him who was Love to die, but behold the spectacle presented to his eye, when he looked into the future to see of the travail, i.e. but a small part of the fruits of his atonement. He beheld the number sealed, of each tribe of Israel 12,000, in all 144,000,—after this he saw, and lo! a great multitude which no man could number, of all nations, and kindreds, and people, and tongues, stood before throne, and before the Lamb, clothed with white robes, and palms in their hands. Already he hears them shout the praises of his death with a loud voice, "salvation to our God which sitteth upon the throne, and unto the Lamb." He is satisfied—he runs with joyful haste, and seizes upon our humanity—cheerfully gives himself up to die to redeem this sacramental Host, and fill heaven with a new and exhaustless theme of praise.

We here repeat our proposition, viz:

That so far as relates to our allegiance and love to

GOD'S SOVEREIGNTY AND FREE MORAL AGENCY - 43

God and the salvation of the world in general, God has purposed and decreed that it shall be through the belief of the truth, none of his acts forcing or compelling the sinner to embrace or reject salvation.

That God may or may not have especial designs of mercy in the ultimate return and salvation of his covenant people Israel, —"we are called in question."

That God displayed especial grace in the conversion and calling of John the Baptist, and the apostles, is evident from the scriptures. The Saviour appeared unto Paul by the way and miraculously convinced him that he was Christ and sent him a vessel of mercy to the Gentiles. But all this is out of ordinary and appointed means of grace. The only hope that remains to us to be saved, is by submitting to the terms of the gospel, viz: "Repentance towards God and faith in our Lord Jesus Christ."

We come to notice the last quibble of one guilty of sleeping on this enchanted ground. "If God foreknew from, all eternity that I would be finally saved or lost, I shall be, and nothing that I can do can alter my destiny."

Very Well. Let us apply this reasoning to something which we can understand.

"If God knew from all eternity, how many barrels of corn or bales of cotton I shall make next year," says the farmer, "I shall raise just so many and nothing that I can do, will make it otherwise," and so he neither plows nor sows. How much corn or tobacco do you think he would raise? He would want in harvest and starve in winter, and sinner, you will just as certainly go down to hell if you rely on the same foolish hope. God does not know that you will make corn or cotton without your exertions, for he could not know a thing that could have no existence— he knows to-day just as well, that you will not be saved without active and energetic efforts on your part, as though the gloom of ten thousand midnights were this moment rolling between your souls and heaven. God does, so far as we know, neither foreknow, or decree anything concerning us, as *moral agents*, and accountable beings, irrespective of our actions, he decrees the consequences of our acts, i.e. he that believeth and is baptised shall be saved, and he that believeth not shall be damned.

From the discussion of this subject

GOD'S SOVEREIGNTY AND FREE MORAL AGENCY

WE LEARN,

1st. That God's absolute will, is the rule of his action, as the sovereign of the universe, and that these acts do not conflict with our accountability, for the accomplishment of this will he does not ask us to pray.

2nd. That God's pleasurable or commanding will is the rule of our acts, and this will is that we should obey the truth and be saved, and he grants us his spirit and grace to help us, if we will accept of them. So if we are lost the guilt lies at our own door, that we may obey God and the world be saved, we should both labor and pray.

4th. We learn why so many are called and so few elected or chosen, because so few will believe the truth, so few are willing to be saved upon the plan by which God has determined to save the lost world.

5th. That, to be a Calvinist, is to be a *fatalist*. For if God pre-determined and decreed, to save a definite number, irrespective of moral character, and reprobated all the rest; irrespective of future moral character, and this certain quantity cannot be increased or diminished, and only this number Christ's death benefited, then the personal and everlasting destiny of each one is *irrevocably* fixed, and no act of the creature can alter it, even though he should believe the truth. The non-elect could not make their election sure, nor could the elect make theirs *less* sure.

6th. To be an [Arminian] is to be a *Universalist*. For if all will be saved for whom Christ died, and he died for *all*, in general, and for *each* in *particular*, then *all* in general, and each in particular must be saved.

7th. That it is our duty to labor and pray that God's will may be done in our own hearts.

8th. In our own families.

9th. In our own neighborhoods and church.

10th. In our own State—in heathen lands.

11th. In proportion as we pray for the salvation of the world, we shall give, even sacrifice to give of our goods to the support of the gospel at home and in heathen lands. May God help us ever thus to pray, to labor and to sacrifice, until the knowledge of the Lord shall cover the earth as the waters cover the channels of the great deep.

The End

www.ingramcontent.com/pod-product-compliance
Lightning Source LLC
Chambersburg PA
CBHW030140100526
44592CB00011B/970